The Mystery
of Faith

THE MYSTERY OF FAITH

An Introduction to Catholicism

MICHAEL J. HIMES

ST. ANTHONY MESSENGER PRESS

Cincinnati, Ohio

Nihil obstat: Rev. Richard W. Walling

Imprimi potest: Fred Link, O.F.M.
Provincial

Imprimatur: Most Rev. Carl K. Moeddel, V. G.
Auxiliary Bishop
Archdiocese of Cincinnati
September 5, 2003

Cover and book design by Mark Sullivan
Cover photo: S. Meltzer/PhotoLink

Library of Congress Cataloging-in-Publication Data

Himes, Michael J.
    The mystery of faith : an introduction to Catholicism / Michael Himes.

      p. cm.
    ISBN 0-86716-579-0
    1. Catholic Church—Doctrines. I. Title.
    BX1751.3.H56 2004
    230'.2—dc22

                                    2003025696

ISBN 0–86716–579–0
Copyright ©2004, Michael Himes
All rights reserved.

Published by St. Anthony Messenger Press
www.AmericanCatholic.org
Printed in the U.S.A.

01 02 03 04 05 06 07 10 9 8 7 6 5 4 3 2 1

TABLE OF CONTENTS

PREFACE

*O*ne of the pleasures and, I must confess, surprises of
the last several years has been the number of times I
have met people who have told me that they have seen
and enjoyed videotapes that I have made. The videotape
series that they mention most often is *The Mystery of
Faith: An Introduction to Catholicism*. I have been aston-
ished and gratified by the number of parishes, schools
and dioceses that use all or parts of that series.

Douglas Fisher, then of Corpus Videos, now of Fisher
Productions, first suggested to me the idea of a number of
videotaped presentations, each of which would be
between twenty and thirty minutes long. The audience
might be varied: participants in a parish education pro-
gram, high school and college students, catechumens
preparing for reception into the church. The presentations would not be complete treatments of the various topics by any means. Rather, each tape was to be an
invitation to consider a subject from perhaps a new

perspective and to encourage conversation about it. The length of the presentation would permit viewing the tape and engaging in some discussion of its content within the space of an hour-long session. Doug's enthusiasm for the project persuaded me to make two videotapes in order to see whether there was an audience for them. Those first two taped presentations were "Trinity" and "Incarnation." (Let it never be said that we did not deal with big issues!) Sometime later Doug reported that he was getting an even more enthusiastic response than he had hoped. We taped a third presentation, "Tradition," to test whether that enthusiasm would continue. It did, and so the other seven videotapes in the series were produced. The format has proved so successful that several others series followed, all of which have continued to be well received and widely used.

At various times since the videotapes first appeared, I have had requests that I publish the texts of the presentations. Many persons and groups who use the series regularly have reported that they would find it helpful to have a text available for reference and reflection. I was reluctant to publish the texts because there were none. One of the goals of the tapes was to convey a sense of someone speaking directly to his audience. To maintain that feel and preserve some spontaneity, I did not lecture from a text; I just spoke to the camera. Whether or not this achieved its purpose, it meant that I had no texts to give to a printer. St. Anthony Messenger Press now publishes all the videotapes that I have done. When Jeremy Harrington, O.F.M., the press's always gracious publisher, urged Doug Fisher to urge me to turn *The Mystery of Faith* series into a book and offered to have the videotapes transcribed so that I had only to edit them, I decided that I could no longer refuse.

I have lightly edited the transcribed texts. This was necessary because, as every teacher and writer knows, the difference between prose to be heard and prose to be read is vast. What makes perfect sense to the ear looks odd to the eye, and vice versa. Also, I have been mindful that many of the requests for these texts came from people who wanted them as a supplement to the videotapes. Comparison with the videotapes will show that I have made two principal changes. The first is that, whereas on the videos I quote Scripture in several different translations, for consistency's sake in the printed texts I have used the *New Revised Standard Version* throughout. The second change is that I have altered several references to "the end of the twentieth century" to "the beginning of the twenty-first century." How time flies when one is enjoying oneself!

I should note once again that this book, like the videotapes from which it comes, is not intended to be a full presentation of the teaching of the Catholic tradition. It is certainly not a catechism. It is, I hope, a collection of interesting and perhaps provocative reflections on major topics in Catholicism. Because the videotapes were designed to be used singly or as a series, each presentation is independent of the others.

Finally, I must express my gratitude to Douglas Fisher, who is most responsible for all the videotapes that we have made together over the years, and to Jeremy Harrington, who is most responsible for this book.

CHAPTER ONE

Trinity

I suppose that no doctrine in the Christian tradition has caused more confusion than the Trinity. But today I fear that, for many people, it is the doctrine that does not make any difference. After all, if someone were to get into the pulpit next Sunday and announce, "We have received a letter from Rome. There has been a change: not three Persons in God, but four," would it really require people to rethink the way they pray, to reevaluate how they live their marriages or bring up their children or make professional decisions? If not, it is tragic. For the Trinity is not one doctrine among others: It is the whole of Christian doctrine. Consider the creed that we recite together Sunday after Sunday at the Eucharist. In the creed we do not say that we believe in one God in three Persons. Rather, we say that we believe in everything else *in terms of* the doctrine of the Trinity: "We believe in one God, the Father who... " and we profess faith in the doctrines of creation and providence, and "in the Son who..." and we state our belief in the doctrines of the incarnation, redemption and resurrection, and "in the Holy Spirit, the Lord and Giver of life, who..." followed by the doctrines of Scripture, tradition, the church and eschatology. In fact, the whole creed is a statement of belief in the Trinity.

And yet it remains a puzzle. What does it mean to say that we believe in one God who, in some way, exists in three Persons? Many people, I suspect, end up thinking of God as a kind of committee (which fortunately consists of an odd number so there can never be a tie vote). Or perhaps we avoid the committee-God by thinking of the Trinity as three ways in which God acts, as though sometimes God acts like the Father, sometimes like the Son and sometimes like the Holy Spirit.

The best statement of the Trinity is found in the New Testament, in the document that we call the First Letter of John. In the fourth chapter at verse 8 and again at verse 16 we read that "God is love." The Greek word for "love" used in this statement is *agape*. Greek has several words that can be translated "love." *Eros* names a love which finds satisfaction in the person or thing loved. *Philia* is companionship or friendship. *Agape,* however, is a very peculiar kind of love. It is a love which is completely centered on the one loved. It is centered on the other. To avoid confusing it with other meanings of "love" in English, I prefer to translate it as "self-gift." So, according to 1 John 4:8 and 16, God is perfect self-gift, total giving of self to the other. Consider this: In the classic Christian definition of the meaning of the word "God," we do not say that God is a lover. Nor do we say that God is one who loves or experiences love or possesses love. We say that God *is* the peculiar kind of love known as *agape,* perfect self-gift. To put this in other words, the First Letter of John claims that if one wants to know how to think about God, God is least wrongly thought of as a particular kind of relationship among persons, specifically the relationship of perfect self-gift. Now, *that* is a remarkable claim: God is least wrongly to be thought of as a relationship, as what happens between and among persons. In fact, that claim appears many times in the collection of earliest Christian documents that we call the New Testament.

For example, the familiar statement attributed to Jesus, "For where two or three are gathered in my name, I am there among them" (Matthew 18:20), should be taken seriously. Jesus does not mean that whenever people come together and think about him, he is with them. What the statement means is that whenever people come together in true mutual love, in genuine concern and care for one another, in short, in *agape*, Jesus will be discovered in what happens among them. To take another example, consider the Last Supper scene in John's Gospel. Jesus delivers his farewell discourse to his disciples (John 13–17). The whole discourse is a meditation on love and community. Surprisingly, Jesus does not tell his disciples to love God. He tells them that they must love one another. Indeed, he says that this will be the hallmark which will distinguish them as his disciples

(John 13:35). Once again, the word used is *agape,* complete gift of self to the other. Jesus tells his hearers that if they love one another agapically, the Father and he will dwell in them. He urges them to continue to live in the love which he and the Father share with one another. Note, please: God is not the object of love; God *is* the love that exists among Jesus' disciples. One discovers the presence of God by discovering the love that unites the community. That is our highest and best experience of God's presence.

Some three centuries after the Fourth Gospel and the First Letter of John were written, Saint Augustine wrote that, while the language of "Father," "Son" and "Spirit" is certainly present in the New Testament (Matthew 28:19), he did not find it the most helpful terminology for teaching about the Trinity. In his great work *On the Trinity* he examines other sets of terms. The best language he comes up with—and I think it is wonderful language—is to speak of God as Lover, Beloved and the Love between them. From all eternity God is the Lover who gives Godself away perfectly; and the Beloved who accepts being loved and returns it perfectly; and the Love, the endless, perfect bond of mutual self-gift uniting the Lover and Beloved. From all eternity God is an enormous explosion of *agape,* self-gift, and it is that self-gift which grounds all that exists. That perfect gift of the divine Self lies at the heart of everything that exists. Therefore, if we are to be like God, we are called to be agapic.

One of the most extraordinary statements of this that I know in the whole Christian tradition is found in Matthew 25:31–46 where we find the Last Judgment described as the separation of sheep from goats. To the sheep on his right hand the Son of Man says,

> Come, you that are blessed by my Father, inherit the kingdom prepared for you from the foundation of the world; for I was hungry and you gave me food, I was thirsty and you gave me something to drink, I was a stranger and you welcomed me, I was naked and you gave me clothing, I was sick and you took care of me, I was in prison and you visited me.

Those on his left are condemned because they did none of these things. Both sides, those who are blessed as well as those who are condemned, respond that they never saw him in those conditions, and the same explanation is given to each: when they cared—or failed to care—for the least of their brothers and sisters, they cared or failed to care for the Son of Man. Please notice: the criterion of judgment has nothing to do with any explicitly *religious* action. The criterion is not whether we were baptized, or prayed, or read Scripture, or received the Eucharist, or believed the correct doctrines, or belonged to the church. Not one of these—however important they may be—is raised as the principle of judgment. Only one criterion is given: Did you love your brothers and sisters? Further, you do not have to love your brothers and sisters because of a conscious reference to the Lord, because even the blessed on the right hand of the Son of Man respond that they had not recognized the Lord in the least of their brothers and sisters, that they had not thought of the Lord when they cared for those in need. The point is that to love the least of our brothers and sisters is to love the Lord, *whether we know it or not.* This is because, at the heart of the gospel, lies one great commandment: that we love one another as Christ has loved us (John 13:34). It is entirely right that this should be the one new commandment Jesus gives us, because the Christian tradition maintains that God *is* love.

Consequently, I think that the ancient Christian hymn which the church sings year after year on Holy Thursday during the *mandatum,* the ritual reenacting of Christ's washing his disciples' feet at the last supper, best summarizes both the central meaning of the doctrine of the Trinity and what the Christian tradition wants to say about the meaning of the word "God": *Ubi caritas et amor, Deus ibi est,* "Wherever there is charity and love, there is God."

For Reflection

- *How has your understanding of the Trinity made a difference in your faith?*

- *What does it mean to say "God is Love"? When have you experienced God as love?*

- *What does the Trinity have to do with love of neighbor?*

CHAPTER TWO

Grace

*F*ew words in the vocabulary of Catholic theology are more important or more ancient than "grace." Over the course of centuries theologians have drawn all sorts of very careful and sometimes helpful distinctions about the meaning of "grace." Perhaps it would be helpful if I offer a straightforward but, I think, all-encompassing definition of the word. By "grace" I mean the love of God outside the Trinity. From all eternity God is pure and perfect self-gift, and the doctrine of the Trinity is a way of exploring the meaning of that statement. When God chooses to give Godself away outside the Trinity, we speak about grace. And what happens when God gives Godself away outside the Trinity? The universe. The universe exists because God loves it completely, perfectly, absolutely at every moment. You and I exist because we are held in being by God. We are loved into existence, and the love of God which lies at the root of all creation, including you and me, is called *grace.* The whole of creation exists because it is engraced. Thus one cannot gain grace or lose grace. If one lost grace, that is, if one ceased to be loved by God, one would not be damned; one would simply not be. The very foundation of being is grace, the pure and perfect love of God. So all creation exists because it is held in being by the action of God who is always self-gift.

This is an important point to keep in mind because it is not only the foundation of our doctrine of creation—that everything is held in being by God's grace—but also the underpinning of everything that the Catholic tradition maintains about sacraments. If everything is loved by God or, to put it another way, if everything is engraced, then somewhere, sometime that grace must be expressed. To give an example: if God is everywhere, how can we speak of certain places as sacred? Whatever we mean when we call a church or a chapel a sacred space, we certainly cannot mean that God is present there but not present in the parking lot next door or at the supermarket or in the bank. If God is present everywhere, what makes the church or a chapel a special, sacred place? The answer is not that God is present there and absent elsewhere, but that, since God is present everywhere, you and I need to notice, accept and celebrate that presence somewhere. So the community sets apart a particular place and calls it sacred.

To take another example: we call Sunday "the Lord's day." Clearly that does not mean that God is unavailable on Tuesdays or takes off on Thursdays. Every day is the

Lord's day. But if all time is God's time, sometime we had better notice the fact. And so the Christian community has traditionally set aside the first day of the week, Sunday, as the Lord's day. We call it sacred time, but the reason we have sacred times and sacred places is that all times and places are God's. God does not require particular times and places as God's unique domain. *We* need them in order to attend to the ever-present grace of God.

This is the heart of what might be called *the sacramental principle,* the heart of the Catholic understanding of the Christian tradition. The sacramental principle might be expressed in this way: If something is always and everywhere the case, it must be noticed, accepted and celebrated somewhere sometime. What is always true must be noticed as true at a particular time and in a particular place. Thus in creation, all of which is grounded in grace, those points—persons, things, places, events, actions—which cause us to notice the presence of grace are what we speak of as sacraments. What can be sacramental? Anything. How many sacraments are there? As many as there are things in existence in the universe. There are, of course, the seven great communal sacraments, those seven special moments in the church's life which the community has set apart as particular celebrations of God's grace. But all of us have personal sacraments: people, things, places or events which speak to us deeply and richly of the love of God which we know surrounds us always but of which we are not always aware. Such particular persons and things and places and events are sacraments *for us,* and sometimes those personal sacraments may be even more effective as signs of grace for us than the great public sacraments. I am sure that each of us has had the experience of attending Mass but finding that, because we were tired or preoccupied or just out of sorts at the time, we did not get as much out of the celebration as we should have. Yet later, when we had the opportunity to be quiet, to take a walk in a place that we really like, to recollect our thoughts, we have found those moments of quiet reflection and prayer to be more effective signs of grace for us on that particular day than the celebration of Mass was. Such moments, personal sacramental moments, may occasionally be more fruitful signs of grace *for us* than the communal celebration of the Eucharist. The whole Catholic tradition can be thought of as a training in becoming sacramental beholders.

The great nineteenth-century English poet, Gerard Manley Hopkins, who was also a Jesuit priest, wrote in one of his poems entitled "Hurrahing in Harvest" of walking one day in the autumn. He was saddened by the passing of summer and the onset of winter; he would miss the beauty of the season that was departing and did not at all look forward to a long, cold winter in Wales where he was teaching. Then he realized that he was lamenting what was gone and fearing what had not yet come but was failing to attend to the present, the moment which actually existed. That recognition enabled him to observe the beauty all around him. Hopkins concludes the poem with the wonderful line, "These things, these things were here and but the beholder/ Wanting." I think that is the most beautiful expression I know of the sacramental principle. The grace of God is here, always here, but what is missing all too often is someone to behold it. Those moments when we become beholders of grace are sacramental moments. All of us are learning to be such beholders. Grace is to be found everywhere.

If this is true, then we cannot make an easy distinction between the sacred and the secular. We cannot divide the world into the realm of grace and the realm of ordinary or natural life. The whole of life is engraced; there is no separate realm of the sacred, no point in our experience, no moment in time, no place in our world which can be set apart as the domain of God as opposed to the rest of our life, the rest of our world, which could then be regarded as merely ordinary life. All life rests on grace. This means that we cannot divide the world into the realms of our actions and God's actions.

No one in the Christian tradition has maintained this more forcefully and more insistently than Thomas Aquinas. Saint Thomas insists again and again throughout his writings that one cannot divide up any event into God's work and our work. Indeed, claims Saint Thomas, it is always a mistake to ask about an event how much of it was caused by God and how much of it can be explained by purely natural causes as if God did part of the work and some natural cause (like us) did the rest. Quite the contrary, everything that happens is caused completely by God and completely by natural agents. (See, for example, *Summa contra Gentiles* 3, 70.) We cannot forget that God is *God*. Saint Thomas constantly insists that we recognize that God is never in competition with God's creatures. God is sovereignly God. God has no competitors. Consequently, God does not act side by side with natural causes; God undergirds all natural causes. God is the cause of there being any other causes.

I can illustrate my point by looking at my hand. I can look at it from the front or from the back, but it remains one hand. "Front" and "back" are perspectives on one reality, one hand. So, too, when we consider the world. There is not a universe of grace and a universe that is merely natural. There is only the one universe. Viewed from one perspective we call it grace; viewed from another perspective we call it nature. There are not two realms, that of grace and nature; there is only the one universe that God calls into being. The difference between grace and nature is not a difference between two separate domains or levels of reality; the difference between nature and grace is a difference of perspective, a matter of how one looks at the world. Thomas Aquinas and many scholastic theologians called this a modal difference. The world under one mode is called grace and under another mode is called nature. The whole world and all that is in it are caused by God, and the whole world and all that is in it are caused by natural causes. It is all natural, but it is also all grace. What changes is how one beholds the world.

So we cannot divide our lives into sacred actions and ordinary or natural actions. Everything we do is a sacred action and a natural action. There is no domain of life that is simply foreign to grace. We cannot say that celebrating the Eucharist is holy but entering a voting booth or shopping in a supermarket or what we do at our work or how we act in our schools and our homes and the marketplace are aspects of life remote from grace. There is no "natural" part of our lives opposed to those "supernatural" moments that are the domain of grace. What we do on Sunday cannot be kept isolated from what we do Monday through Saturday. We do not live in two realms. We live in one realm that can be regarded from two perspectives.

The English poet William Blake wrote, "Twofold always. May God us keep / From single vision and Newton's sleep."[1] Blake warned us never to fall into the mistake of looking at the world from one line of vision, one perspective, simply seeing the world as a play of natural forces. That, he thought, was the mistake of the Newtonian science of his time, "Newton's sleep," as he termed it. We must see reality from two perspectives. The world is both totally God's and totally natural. The world is held in being at every moment by God's action. We must understand this about ourselves. We cannot parcel out our lives into the natural and the supernatural. All life is supernaturally grounded. All life is built on grace. This profoundly affects our understanding of the church's mission. The church is not a community which seeks to lead people from the level of nature to the level of grace or supernature. The church is the community that witnesses to the graced reality of the world. Thus the church is not an isolated realm of grace in a profane or secular world. Rather, the church is the revelation of what is true of the whole world. The church is not the

[1] Included in a letter to Thomas Butts, November 22, 1802, in Geoffrey Keynes, ed., *Complete Prose and Poetry of William Blake* (London: The Nonesuch Press, 1989), p. 862.

community of those who are loved by God in the midst of a world which is not loved by God, an island of grace in an ungraced world. Because the whole world is engraced, the church is a sacrament, a revelation, a moment in which the reality of the whole world comes to the surface and can be clearly seen—or, at least, should be clearly seen. The church's mission is not to say to the world, "Come and be what we are and then you will be engraced." Rather, the church's mission is to announce to the world, "You are already engraced. Aren't you delighted? Come and celebrate with us." The church is the sacrament of the meaning of the world.

The sacred is the sacramental form of the secular. Grace underlies all of nature. You and I can accept grace more fully or, tragically, we can reject grace. But what we cannot do is fall out of grace, because grace is the love of God outside the Trinity. We may accept or reject that love, but nothing we can do can prevent God from loving us. The love of God is always present. Grace is everywhere.

For Reflection

- *Grace is the "love of God outside the Trinity." What does this mean?*

- *If grace is present everywhere, what makes the church and sacraments sacred?*

- *How can you increase your awareness of grace? How is the work you do sacred?*

CHAPTER THREE
Incarnation

*T*he most remarkable statement about the Incarnation
in the Christian tradition is found right at the beginning
of the tradition. In the second chapter of his letter to the
church in Philippi, Saint Paul cites a hymn which pre-
dates his letter and therefore is very close in time to
Jesus' life, death and resurrection. Quoting the hymn, he
writes of Christ:

> [W]ho, though he was in the form of God,
> did not regard equality with God
> as something to be exploited,
> but emptied himself,
> taking the form of a slave,
> being born in human likeness.
> And being found in human form,

he humbled himself,
and became obedient to the point of death—
even death on a cross. (Philippians 2:6–8)

Think about that for a moment. Paul claims not just that
we are like Christ but that Christ has chosen to be one
with us rather than remaining in the form of God. This
is, without question, the most extraordinary compliment
ever paid to being human. And that, after all, is what the
incarnation is really about. It is not, first and foremost,
the revelation of who God is; first and foremost, it is the
revelation of who we are. The Incarnation tells us what
it is to be a human being.

But precisely what does it tell us about being a
human being? Let me suggest that it continues a theme
that is very deeply grounded within Israel's tradition.
From a time many centuries before the appearance of
Christianity, in the first chapter of the book of Genesis,
we read that on the afternoon of the sixth day (because,
in the story, God will take time off on the seventh day,
this is the end of the process of creation) God creates the
climax, the high point of all creation, that to which
everything has been building—human beings. In
describing how God creates human beings, the pattern of
the first five days of the week of creation is broken. In
the familiar story of Genesis, the pattern on each of the
first five days of creation has been that God says, "Let
there be..." something, and that something comes into
being (Genesis 1:3, 6, 9, 11, 14, 20, 24), and God looks at
what has been created and sees that it is good. For the
first time on the afternoon of the sixth day, however,

God is depicted as deliberating before creating. God determines to make the human being in God's own image and likeness. For the first time God does not just say, "Let it happen," and it happens. God pauses to plan what is about to be done and uses a blueprint for this all-important creature, the blueprint being Godself. This introduces an important theme in the Hebrew tradition. Later in the Mosaic law we find the strong insistence that we not make any idols or images of God (Exodus 20:4; Deuteronomy 5:8). The word translated as *idol* in those prohibitions is the same word translated as *image* in Genesis when we are told that we are the image and likeness of God. That is why Israel did not think it possible to make an image of God. It was redundant: God had already made an image of Godself, and we are it.

In the third chapter of Genesis we find the story of the fall of Adam and Eve. You recall that the temptation which the serpent presents to the first human beings is not disobedience, nor is it pride. The temptation is that if they eat the forbidden fruit they will become like God. That may be the most important line that evil is given in the Scriptures: Eat this and be like God. The temptation, you will observe, is to reject what we have learned. In the first chapter of Genesis we heard that we have been made in the image and likeness of God. In chapter three the serpent's temptation is, in effect, "Don't believe that you're like God. How can *you* be like *God*? God is great and glorious and powerful and majestic and wise; you're not like *that*. Being human is a messy business. You don't want to be human. You have to abandon being human in order to be like God." The origin of sin, according to the

Hebrew tradition, is the rejection of the goodness of being human. It arises from the insistence that we human beings are not the image and likeness of God, that we must become something other than and more than human beings in order to truly be like God. In other words, according to the Hebrew Scriptures, the first sin—the entry of evil into creation—is the refusal to accept the goodness and rightness of being human. Evil is the refusal to accept the goodness of creation. To put it slightly differently, the sin which is the origin of all evil in the world is the rejection of God's first judgment on us: "God saw everything that he had made, and indeed, it was very good" (Genesis 1:31). In contrast, the serpent insists that creation is not good at all; creation—including you and me—is trash. The acceptance of the serpent's judgment rather than God's is what leads to all the evil in history. The beginning of sin is despair of the goodness of creation.

This is "the mystery that was kept secret for long ages but is now [as the prophets wrote] disclosed" (Romans 16:25–26)—the extraordinary claim of the hymn quoted in Philippians 2. God did not see being divine as something to be clung to; God emptied Godself and took on humanity, becoming like us in all things except sin. Let me put this another way: The great mystery hidden from all generations and revealed in the Incarnation is God's secret ambition. From all eternity God has wanted to be exactly like you and me. This is the ultimate statement of the goodness of being human, the rightness of humanity. The immense dignity of the human person is at the heart of the Christian tradition because it flows directly from the doctrine of the Incarnation itself. Indeed, the Incarnation is the highest compliment ever paid to being human. It is also the divine response to our original sin. If the originating sin, the origin of evil, is the rejection of the goodness of being a human being, the Incarnation is the unsurpassable revelation of that goodness.

When in the New Testament we read that Jesus has become like us in all things except sin (see Hebrews 4:15), we are taught that our humanity is what now unites us with the fullness of God's glory. Let us consider that for a moment. One of the great images for this claim is the doctrine of the Ascension. I sometimes think that the feast of the Lord's Ascension is one of the most poorly celebrated of the great liturgical days in the liturgical calendar. Unfortunately we have made it into a divine "bon voyage" party, as if we are honoring Jesus' departure from earth. But surely the point is not that Jesus has left us and gone back to where he was before. Rather, the point is that the one who has ascended into heaven and who now, in the traditional imagery of the creed, sits at the right hand of the Father in glory is a human being exactly like us in all things except sin. What unites us with the fullness of the glory of the Father, therefore, is our humanity. God and you and I have one thing in common: humanity. That is what the doctrine of the Incarnation is really about. Consequently, if there is anything that the Christian tradition must emphasize, it is the immense dignity, value and importance of genuine, full and authentic humanity because it is by being fully and authentically human, by being as human as we can possibly be, that you and I become more fully and truly like God or, to put it another way, that we become holy. Any form of spirituality that belittles humanity, that de-emphasizes the goodness and dignity of the human person, must be regarded by Christians as an obstacle to genuine union with God. Thus, any work which furthers the dignity of the human person is also a work of sanctification, a work of holiness.

In Vatican II's *Dogmatic Constitution on the Church* (*Lumen Gentium*) we read that the church "is in Christ as a sacrament or instrumental sign of intimate union with God and of the unity of all of humanity" (LG 1,1). A very distinguished Catholic theologian, Nicholas Lash, has suggested that sometimes in theology the most interesting and important word in a doctrinal statement is "and."[2] I think that is true in this statement from Vatican II. The church is a sacrament or instrumental sign of intimate union with God *and* of the unity of all of humanity. The church is called to be a sacrament of two realities that are intimately linked. This statement in *Lumen Gentium*, which has become an important description of the church and its ministry, is, in fact, a recapturing of a very ancient Christian insight. Recall that, in Mark's Gospel, Jesus, when asked by a scribe what the first commandment is, replies by seemingly citing two familiar commandments. One must love God

[2] Nicholas Lash, *His Presence in the World: A Study in Eucharistic Worship and Theology* (London: Sheed and Ward, 1968), p. 4f: "It therefore becomes clear that the real difficulty in saying that Christianity, or theology, is about both God and man, the real difficulty in verus Deus et verus homo, consists not in knowing what we mean by God or what we mean by man (though these are not small questions), but in the difficulty of knowing what we mean by and."

with one's whole mind, heart and soul, he tells the scribe, and one must love one's neighbor as oneself. When the scribe responds, "You are right, Teacher; you have truly said that 'he is one, and besides him there is no other'; and 'to love him with all the heart, and with all the understanding, and with all the strength', and 'to love one's neighbor as oneself,'—this is much more important than all whole burnt offerings and sacrifices," Jesus tells him, "You are not far from the kingdom of God" (Mark 12:28–34). What elicits this praise from Jesus—the single greatest compliment the Lord pays to anyone in Mark's Gospel—is that the scribe recognized that Jesus had not dodged his question by citing two commandments. Rather, Jesus gave one commandment but said it in two ways. To love God completely and to love one's neighbor as oneself are one and the same thing. I suggest that this is the meaning of "and" in the statement from Vatican II's *Lumen Gentium*: intimate union with God and the unity of all of humanity are the same thing. One cannot be in intimate union with God—which is as good a definition of holiness as any I know—without simultaneously striving in unity with all of humanity for the common good. The two go hand-in-hand because the dignity of humanity is at the heart of the gospel. An insistence on reverence for all of humanity and for oneself as part of humanity flows from the Incarnation as the center of our faith. Only in recognizing the intrinsic dignity, value and worth of oneself and of all other human beings can one genuinely love God.

This has been powerfully said by a well-known Roman Catholic theologian who wrote some years ago that Christianity is an attitude of "deep amazement at the human person's worth and dignity." Astonishing—a definition of Christianity that does not mention God! This theologian does not define Christianity as the love of God, or the worship of God, or belief in God, but rather as the attitude of amazement before the dignity of the human person. Perhaps someone may say that one can find theologians who will say anything these days. This well-known Roman Catholic theologian, however, is Pope John Paul II in his first encyclical, *Redemptor Hominis.*[3] The pope's statement captures something absolutely central to our faith. Indeed, were I to sum it up in a single phrase, I doubt that I could do better than the words of Saint Irenaeus, a second-century father of the church, who wrote that "the glory of God is a human being fully alive." This claim of Irenaeus is deeply rooted in the Christian doctrine of the Incarnation: the insistence that the one who was in the form of God did not think equality with God was anything to be clung to but emptied Godself and became like us in all things except sin. If we are to be like God we must be fully human, because God has chosen to become like us.

---

[3] John Paul II, *Redemptor Hominis* (Washington, D.C.: United States Catholic Conference, 1979), #10, p. 28: "In reality, the name for that deep amazement at the human person's worth and dignity is the Gospel, that is to say: the Good News. It is also called Christianity." As the translation of *hominis* I have substituted for "man" the more accurate "human person," which also has the advantage of being gender-inclusive.

For Reflection

- *"The glory of God is humanity fully alive." What does this mean? When are you fully alive?*

- *How does a true belief in the Incarnation, in the awesome dignity of humanity, change the world? How does this understanding affect your life?*

- *If God were to come again today, what form do you think God would take?*

CHAPTER FOUR
Salvation

*O*ne of the most familiar stories in the western world is also one of the most ancient: the story of Adam and Eve found in the third chapter of Genesis. To understand this familiar story it is important to put it in the context of the first two chapters of Genesis. The very first thing we hear about human beings is that God has made us in God's own image and likeness and that when God looked at us God saw that we were good (Genesis 1:26–27, 31). That is the context within which one has to hear the temptation by the serpent: Eat this and be like God. The serpent's claim is that if the first human beings eat the fruit of the tree from which they have been forbidden to eat they will become like God. What precisely is the temptation here? It is not a temptation to disobedience; that would trivialize the story. I suggest that the real

29

temptation is not to believe what we have heard about ourselves in the first chapter of Genesis. We have heard that human beings are made in God's image and likeness, and two chapters later we find the serpent telling us, in effect, "No, you're not like God. You must do something to become like God. Now you're a mess; you're junk. You must make yourself valuable, and to do so, you will have to pull yourself up by your bootstraps if you are to be like God. Don't believe that God has made you like God." In short, the first temptation is not to believe in the goodness of being human. The first temptation is despair. This is one of the most profound and wisest insights in the Hebrew and Christian traditions: the recognition that evil enters the world through despair, which is the refusal to accept the goodness, the rightness, the blessedness of one's own being as a creature. Evil is the denial of the goodness of being finite. It is the refusal to believe that we are like God.

The Genesis story of the emergence of evil in the world that God has created good was designed to answer a huge problem: where does evil come from? In the ancient world polytheists, people who believed in many gods, had no intellectual problem with evil. The good gods are responsible for good things and the bad gods are responsible for the bad things. It was an easy and straightforward answer to the problem of evil. Evil becomes an intellectual problem, however, if, like the people of Israel, you believe in one God who is all-powerful, responsible for all that exists, and who is good. Where, then, does evil come from? How can evil appear in the universe if God, who creates everything, is good? The problem has been summed up in a jingle by the American poet Archibald MacLeish in his play *J.B.,* his retelling of the Book of Job: "If God is God He is not good, / If God is good He is not God." The jingle's point is that if God is God, i.e., the author of everything, then God must be the author of evil and so cannot be good. On the other hand, if God is good, then God cannot be the author of evil; but in that case God is not the author of everything and so is not really God. This was the dilemma that faced ancient Israel. Ancient Israel's response to the dilemma is that evil does not come from God; it comes from us when we reject ourselves and refuse to accept the goodness of our own being. Evil is despair.

It is an old observation among opera lovers that, in any opera in which he is a character, "the devil gets all the best tunes." One can say much the same thing about Milton's great epic poem, *Paradise Lost.* The best poetry, the most exciting and memorable lines are given to Satan. I think this is because Milton envisions Satan as a monster of pride, as if the source of evil is vanity or self-assertion. With all respect to Milton, I think Dante has a more profound view in *The Divine Comedy.* When Virgil leads Dante to the gate of hell, he finds the inscription carved over the portal, "Abandon all hope, you who enter here" (*Inferno* Canto 3, l. 9). Dante has gotten it precisely right: the entry to hell is hopelessness, despair. When Dante and Virgil finally come face to face with Satan in the lowest pit of hell, we find that Satan is no tragic hero as he sometimes seems to be in Milton's epic, shaking his fist at the heavens and declaring, "Better to reign in hell, than serve in heaven" (Book 1, l. 263). Satan is locked in ice made from his own tears which are frozen by the beating of his wings as he endlessly but vainly tries to free himself. There is a vision of evil: Satan locked in ice, weeping. The heart of hell, Dante knows, is icy despair. I think he understood evil in a more profound way than Milton.

To cite one more great poet, Goethe tells the story in *Faust* of a man who sells his soul to the devil. In Part One, when he summons the demon Mephistopheles, Faust demands to know who he is. Mephistopheles replies in what are, in my opinion, the most chilling lines about evil: "I am the spirit who says No. And that rightly, for all things that are deserve to come to an end. Better there should never have been anything" (ll. 1338–1341). Recall Saint Paul: Jesus Christ "was not 'Yes and No'; but in him it is always 'Yes'" (2 Corinthians 1:19). In the demon Mephistopheles there is no "Yes and No"; his nature is all "No." No to what? No to everything. Is there reason for hope? No. Value to existence? No. Any point in living tomorrow? No. Anything to be expected that would be valuable or good or pleasant? No. Any worth in you? No. In me? No. In Mephistopheles? No. Is there any reason to exist at all? No. All things that are deserve to come to an end, literally, to be *finite*. And therefore they are all trash. "Better there should never have been anything." Goethe's insight is that evil says no to being. God says, "Let there be light" (Genesis 1:3). Evil responds, "No! Let there be darkness." It denies the value of being at all. Either you are God or you ought not to be. Either you are everything or you are nothing.

What is not infinite, what is merely finite, should never have been at all. What Dante and Goethe realized was that Satan is not a monster of pride; Satan is a monster of despair. Satan does not think he is everything; Satan is convinced that he is nothing and ought not exist. Satan does not hate God; Satan refuses to believe that God could possibly love him. That evil arises in despair, that it is the rejection of the goodness of finite being, that it is an irrational insistence on the worthlessness of everything, that it is our conviction that we ought not to be—that is what the Hebrew and Christian traditions see as the heart of darkness.

You may very well find yourself thinking, "How exaggerated!" After all, how often does one find oneself actually willing one's own non-existence? How often does one truly despair of the goodness of one's own being? The answer is, "Probably a great deal more than any of us would like to admit." To be sure, we do not often do so explicitly. But are there not moments when you have been so disappointed with yourself, so discouraged by failure, so embarrassed by your weakness, that if for one instant you had the power to blot everything out rather than confront that weakness or failure, you would have done it? If you have experienced such moments, I think you know how accurate Goethe's description of evil is.

That is precisely what the third chapter of Genesis describes: the temptation not to accept the goodness of being finite and so the goodness of being human. In many ways the whole course of salvation history from the fall of Adam and Eve until the coming of Jesus is the story of God's constant repetition of his original judgment on creation in general and humanity in particular: God looked at us and saw that we were good (Genesis 1:31). Sadly, it is also the story of our repeated refusal to accept that judgment. By refusing to accept the goodness of being human we find ourselves more and more separated from one another. The result of the sin of Adam and Eve is separation from God. In the next generation, the result of Cain's sin in murdering his brother Abel is that human beings cannot trust one another (Genesis 4:1–16). Human beings become separated from one another. The result of the sin of the builders of the tower of Babel is that human beings find themselves living in mutually alienated communities, a separation symbolized by their inability to speak to one another anymore (Genesis 11:1–9). As sin grows in the world we constantly become more alone, more alienated, more separated from God and from one another in ever more separated communities. The attempt to become God ends up depriving us of the ability to be human.

This is the context in which Christianity proclaims the good news of salvation. What is that good news? Saint Paul writes of "the mystery that was kept secret for long ages but is now disclosed" (Romans 16:25–26). The mystery turns out to be what I have described as God's secret ambition. God thinks that being human is so good, so wonderful, that God has chosen to become one. The great irony is that while we have been engaged in a mad and destructive quest to stop being human and become God, God has chosen to become what we are. The one who was in the form of God did not think that being equal to God was anything to be grasped but emptied himself, becoming human like all other human beings (Philippians 2:6–7). The good news is that God has taken on humanity along with us.

Salvation is the story of God's entry into the world in order to reaffirm the first judgment, which is that God has looked at us and seen that we are good. This time we must believe and accept that judgment. We are saved when we agree with God that being human is good. Salvation is not the story of God's rescuing us from an evil universe but of God's coming to live in the universe with us so that we finally recognize how good the universe is.

Recognizing the goodness of the universe is not easily done. In the course of human history we have done a great deal to deface that goodness. When absolute love enters our world in human form in the person of Jesus of Nazareth, we kill him. This is the double significance of the cross. The first thing the cross reveals is the depth of evil in the world. It is so deep that the world's response to perfect love is to try and kill it. The second part of the message of the cross, however, is that absolute love will even embrace death because of its acceptance of the goodness of creation. "Father, forgive them; they do not know what they are doing" (Luke 23:34). When that is said, Jesus can say that "it is finished" (John 19:30). What is finished? Jesus himself is finished. Everything that he can give has been given; there is nothing left to give. Jesus is like a sponge that has been wrung out; every drop has been drained. And because everything that he is has been given away, he cannot be dead. The tomb cannot hold him. That is the great Christian proclamation of salvation. It does not make light of the evil of the world. It recognizes the depth and reality of that evil and then, in embracing it, overcomes it. It insists that life is bigger than death, that love is greater than hatred, that goodness is far deeper than evil. It maintains that evil is a distortion, a parasitic growth on the goodness of creation, that evil is that which should not be. It embraces creation, and therefore shows us once again the goodness of all creation, including humanity.

How can we embrace and accept salvation? In two ways intimately related to one another. First, we must affirm the goodness of who we are. I have often told people that the fundamental statement of salvation has two clauses, and we have to say both with equal strength. The statement is: I am not God, and that is good. The first way in which I embrace salvation is to recognize that I am finite, that I am not God, that I am dependent, and to accept that as good, to celebrate my finiteness, to rejoice in my creatureliness. Second, I must embrace your creatureliness. It is not enough for me to accept the deep goodness of my being; I have to accept the deep goodness of your being. Salvation is always within a community. Only by mutual love, mutual respect, the celebration of one another's goodness as human beings, can salvation be truly accepted. I need to agree with God's judgment not only on me, but on you. God has looked at *us* and seen that *we* are good. Only within a community can we begin to undo the alienation which is the result of evil. The fruit of sin is separation from God and from one another. Consequently salvation reconciles us with one another and so restores us to communion with God. We cannot celebrate salvation outside community. If we accept the good news of salvation, we must enter into communion with one another. There is no salvation without entry into community. There is no salvation without church.

For Reflection

- *When have you witnessed evil separating people?*

- *What does it mean to be saved? How does the cross save us?*

- *How do we embrace salvation?*

CHAPTER FIVE
Church

Sometimes the most obvious questions are the ones that we presume we know the answers to without ever really having addressed them. One such obvious question for many Christians and certainly for most Catholics is, "Why do we need a church?" Why isn't my Christian faith simply a matter between God and me? Why isn't it simply a story about my relationship to God? Why does being a Christian believer require my having a relationship with other human beings? Why should there be a communal dimension to Christianity? In short, why do we need a church? I think there are two reasons especially that we need a church. The first reason is that Christianity is not about timeless truths, not a set of claims about the way the world is and always has been. To be sure, such claims are implied in Christianity, but, first and foremost, Christianity is a story about particular events that happened to particular people in a particular place at a particular time.

Some of the most important—and peculiar—verses in the whole of the New Testament are the first verses of the third chapter of the Gospel of Luke. After the stories of Jesus' birth and growing up are recounted in the first two chapters, the Gospel of Luke turns to Jesus' public ministry by setting the time and place: "In the fifteenth year of the reign of Emperor Tiberius, when Pontius Pilate was governor of Judea, and Herod was ruler of Galilee, and his brother Philip ruler of the region of Ituraea and Trachonitis, and Lysanias ruler of Abilene, during the high priesthood of Annas and Caiaphas, the word of God came to John son of Zechariah in the wilderness" (Luke 3:1–2). What, you may ask, is so interesting and so peculiar about those verses? They are the antithesis of "Once upon a time." They tell us that the story we are about to hear in Luke's Gospel is not a tale of timeless truths. It is a story about particular people who lived at a particular place in a particular time. There is only one way that you and I can know about particular events that occurred in a particular place at a particular time in the past: someone has told us about it. Christianity is not a series of conclusions that any one of us could have reached by simply sitting down and thinking about them very seriously and carefully for a long time. Christianity is a report, a *Gospel,* "good news," and news requires that someone bring the news to us. The first reason that a community of persons is intrinsic to Christianity is that we need to hear the news from someone else. This is, of course, true in our own experience. I first heard the Gospel from my parents. All of us heard the Gospel from others—parents, teachers, pastors, families, friends and relatives. All of us have received the Gospel as a gift from other people. No one arrives at the truth of Christianity by herself or himself.

The second and perhaps even more important reason why Christianity can only be experienced within a community is that Christianity claims that my relationship to God is dependent on my relationship to my brothers and sisters. Now, that is a very striking claim indeed. To illustrate it consider a familiar story from the synoptic gospels. In Matthew's Gospel (22:34–40) a scribe, presumably someone learned in the Mosaic law, asks Jesus a question in order, so the gospel tells us, to trip him up, to make him look foolish, to show that he does not have the knowledge or the credentials to be regarded as a rabbi. So the scribe asks Jesus a much debated question in Judaism in Jesus' time: of all of the hundreds of commandments that the great rabbis had discerned within the Mosaic law over the course of centuries, which one was to be regarded as the most important, the primary, the basic commandment from which all the others flowed? One opinion held that it was to love the Lord your God with your whole mind and your whole heart and your whole strength and your whole being. Another opinion was that the foundational commandment was to love your neighbor as yourself. So the scribe asks Jesus what, in his opinion, is the most important commandment. Apparently the scribe assumed that Jesus would give some inadequate and confused answer, after which his hearers would see that he did not know the law well enough to be regarded as a teacher. Jesus simply combines the two often-cited opinions: Love God with your whole mind, heart and being, he replies, and the second commandment is similar to it: love your neighbor as yourself. That is Matthew's account of the incident.

Luke's Gospel takes the story considerably further (10:25–37). Once again a scribe asks Jesus the question to test him. In this account Jesus responds by turning the question back to the scribe: "What is written in the law? What do you read there?" The scribe replies that one must love God with your whole mind, heart and being and one's neighbor as oneself. To this Jesus answers, "You have given the right answer; do this, and you will live." The scribe does not intend to let Jesus off the hook that easily, and so he demands, "And who is my neighbor?" Jesus responds by telling the parable of the Good Samaritan. Unquestionably the primary point of the parable is that one's neighbor is everyone who is in need. There are no boundaries to who my neighbor is. My neighbor is not limited by race or religious belief or national origin. But there is also a second and more subtle point to the Good Samaritan story, perhaps, in relation to the question the scribe originally asked about the two commandments, a more important point. Recall that in the parable two people pass by the man who was attacked by the robbers and left bleeding by the side of the road, a priest and a Levite who are hurrying on their way to Jerusalem. Presumably, since both have responsibilities in the liturgy, they are on their way to Jerusalem to worship in the temple. That is why the parable pointedly notes that they passed the wounded man by "on the other side of road": they had to make certain that they would not come into contact with any blood, for that would render them unclean and make them unable to worship in the temple. By contrast, when the Samaritan, who does not worship in the temple at Jerusalem at all, comes along, he can help the robber's victim. Notice that at least part of the parable's point is that, if you think that worshiping God is more important then helping your neighbor, you do not know what it means to worship God. Jesus' story is part of his reply to the scribe's original question, and that reply is that anyone who thinks that the commandment to love God and the commandment to love our neighbor are in competition with one another misunderstands both.

Mark's version of the story about the two great commandments is perhaps the most interesting one (12:28–34). In this account the scribe asks Jesus his question not in order to test him up or to demonstrate his incompetence but because he sincerely wants to know what Jesus thinks. So he asks, "Which commandment is the first of all?" Jesus responds that we must love God with our whole mind and heart and being and that the second commandment is identical to it, that we love our neighbor as we love ourselves. The scribe then says, "You are right, Teacher," that indeed nothing is more important then loving God and there is no sacrifice or offering in the temple to be compared with loving our neighbor. To this Jesus answers, "You are not far from the kingdom of God." Mark ends the story with the significant statement, "And after that no one dared to ask him any question." So this is the story that concludes Jesus' teaching in Mark's Gospel. After this there is nothing left to say. Why? What is so important about the conversation between Jesus and the scribe in Mark's Gospel? I suggest that the key to understanding the exchange is that the scribe recognizes that Jesus has not dodged his question: which is the first commandment? At first hearing it may seem that Jesus gives two answers to the question. The point is, however, that the second answer is identical to the first. The scribe wisely acknowledges this. He is saying, in effect, "Well done, Rabbi! You did not give two answers; rather, you said one thing but in two ways." And Jesus' response to the scribe is, "If you know that I said the same thing in two forms, that loving God and loving your neighbor are one and the same, then you are very close to the kingdom of God." I suggest that this enormously important insight in Mark's Gospel finds an even more radical expression in John's Gospel.

John's Gospel has no story that corresponds to the synoptic tale about a scribe posing the question of the great commandments to Jesus. Rather, in John's Gospel at the start of the Last Supper, after Jesus has washed his disciples' feet, we hear that he told his disciples, "I give you a new commandment, that you love one another. Just as I have loved you, you also should love one another. By this everyone will know that you are my disciples" (13:34–35). Perhaps we might wonder: If the great commandment is that we love *one another*, what has happened to the commandment to love *God*? The answer offered by John's Gospel is very profound: "Those who love me will keep my word [the new commandment to love one another], and my Father will love them, and we will come to them and make our home with them" (14:23). John's Gospel teaches us that God is not an object of our love, but rather the very source and ground of our ability to love one another. When we love one another we are experiencing the presence of God. That, I suggest to you, is the deepest reason for the existence of the church. We cannot possibly love God without loving one another because it is only in loving one another that we find out what the word "God" means. We cannot possibly claim to love God and be out of communion with one another. The more profound, the richer, the wider, the deeper, the more embracing the community, the better our experience of mutual love, the deeper our commitment to one another, the greater is our experience of God. It is impossible to love God without loving our neighbor because it is in loving our neighbor that we love God. This extraordinary insistence on the part of Christianity is why the Christian gospel can never be reduced to a private experience between God and me. I cannot find God outside a relationship to all my brothers and sisters. Thus, the church is not simply the bearer of the Christian mysteries. The church's role is not merely to tell us about the mysteries of Christian faith; rather, living in the church is itself a mystery of the Christian faith. Our capacity to live together as a community of people with mutual forgiveness and deep concern for the well being of all members of the community and our desire to spread that community to all our brothers and sisters are the ways in which we come to know what the word "God" means. Isn't that precisely what the first letter of John says in very strong terms? "Those who say, 'I love God,' and hate their brothers or sisters, are liars; for those who do not love a brother or sister whom they have seen, cannot love God whom they have not seen" (1 John 4:20). Not only does such a person distort the truth, he or she could not even know what the word "God" means because the only way in which one can discover who God is, is through one's experience of community. And that is what the church provides us—a community of persons who attempt to live the mystery of God together.

One question that the ancient church confronted about the Christian community was, "What does it mean to say that this church is holy?" We still say when we recite the creed that we believe in one *holy,* catholic and apostolic church. How can the church be called holy? Some people in the ancient church answered—and I fear some people in the church at the present time still think—that the holiness of the church stems from the holiness of its members. Thus the church is holy because it is populated by saints. That means anyone who is not a saint had better get out. Such an understanding of the church has been a temptation all through the church's history. We might call it the puritan temptation. It misses the deepest level of the church's holiness, for, as Saint Augustine pointed out, the real source of the church's holiness is the Holy Spirit. All holiness flows from God's Spirit, and the first effect of the Spirit of God is communion. For example, in the account in the Acts of the Apostles of the Spirit's descent on the earliest Christians at Pentecost (2:1–11), the first sign of the Spirit's presence is that people who come from many different countries hear the gospel proclaimed in their own languages. The separation from one another that resulted from the attempt to build the tower of Babel (Genesis 11:1–9), after which people could no longer speak to one another, is undone when the Spirit comes. The first effect of the Spirit is unity.

So, too, in the Gospel of John's account of the coming of the Spirit on the evening of the Resurrection when Jesus appeared in the upper room to the Eleven who had locked the door for fear of being set upon by the authorities who had executed Jesus. Jesus' first words to the Eleven are, "Peace be with you." Then he breathes on them and says, "Receive the Holy Spirit. If you forgive the sins of any, they are forgiven them; if you retain the sins of any, they are retained" (20:19–23). The first effect of the coming of the Spirit according to John's Gospel is that we can forgive one another, that whatever has separated us from one another can now be healed. In both the Acts of the Apostles and in the Gospel of John the same point is being made: the Spirit unites. The Spirit is the one who brings together those who have been separated. Therefore, Augustine concluded, if the presence of the Spirit who is the source of holiness is marked by communion, the holiness of the church consists not in excluding sinners but in welcoming them. The sign of the church's holiness is not that all its members are morally perfect. The real sign of the church's holiness is that the imperfect people who make up the church can live together without cutting one another's throats. That perfect people live together in peace is no miracle. But that a collection of thoroughly imperfect people can live together over the course of centuries without murdering one another can only be explained as the work of God's Spirit. That is the sign of the Spirit's presence.

So, I suggest, the church is most itself, it most fully lives its mission and fulfills its role in God's plan of salvation, not by excluding anyone but by including everyone who wants to be included. The church is about *inclusion* not exclusion, about *communication* not excommunication. The church brings us together, and in coming together we discover what it means to love God. The church not only tells us the story of Jesus of Nazareth. It provides us with the experience that enables us to understand who it is that Jesus called "Father."

For Reflection

- *What does the word "church" mean to you? How is the church about inclusion, rather than exclusion?*

- *What person was the most significant in bringing the Good News to you? To whom have you brought the Good News?*

- *We love God by loving our neighbor. Have you ever felt tempted to love God and bypass loving your neighbor? When?*

CHAPTER SIX

Baptism

*I*n his letter to the church in Rome, Saint Paul uses language that at first glance seems exaggerated. He writes, "Do you not know that all of us who have been baptized into Christ Jesus were baptized into his death? Therefore we have been buried with him by baptism into death, so that, just as Christ was raised from the dead by the glory of the Father, so we too might walk in newness of life" (Romans 6:3–4). Doesn't it seem odd that when Saint Paul wants to write about Baptism, he describes it as an experience of dying and being raised from the dead? We have heard this kind of language so often and the passage from the letter to the Romans is so familiar to us that perhaps the imagery no longer strikes us as strange. But consider: when the Christian community describes the process, the event, the celebration by which new members enter the community, it does so in the language of death and resurrection. I suspect that most people do not think of the commitment that we made—or in the case of many Catholics, that our parents and godparents made for us—as a matter of life and death. But our earliest brothers and sisters in the Christian community did think of it in precisely that way. After all, for almost the first three hundred years of Christian history, entering the community was literally an act that put one's life on the line. It was a capital crime in the Roman empire to declare oneself a Christian believer, so when our earliest brothers and sisters in the faith were baptized, they faced death as an all-too-possible result.

In addition to the possibility of execution, those early believers faced another kind of death in joining the Christian community because they were radically changing their entire way of life prior to baptism. When they entered the community they broke with the customs, the family traditions, the social and economic conditions that had previously shaped their lives. We still possess a list that was drawn up in the early third century of occupations which the Christian community regarded as acceptable for its members. There were many occupations closed to Christians which seem innocuous to us at first glance, so many that one might well wonder how the early Christians ever managed to make a living. Classical paganism was so well established that virtually every aspect of life was connected to pagan religion. For example, Christians of the time thought that those who wished to enter their community could not be painters or sculptors, presumably because the commissions that such artists would receive would likely involve depicting pagan gods and goddesses or mythological stories. Christians, they thought, ought not to be architects, probably because important architectural commissions would involve designing and constructing temples for pagan worship. Teaching was not a recommended occupation, because teachers would be expected to educate their students in classical pagan literature and that, of course, would require expounding pagan myths. Similarly, a Christian could not be an actor or in any way connected with the theater since actors performed plays based on classical mythology. A Christian could not even be a butcher because butcher shops in ancient cities were usually attached to pagan temples (one had to do something with all those sacrificed animals). It is easy to imagine how upset pagan parents would be when their children who had become Christians told them they could no longer attend family celebrations of anniversaries and births and deaths since such events often involved sacrifices to the pagan gods and other non-Christian religious rituals. Think how family members must have felt when a son or a daughter, a brother or a sister, a wife or a husband became a Christian and refused to attend family celebrations or take part in family holidays. I suppose they responded the way most people today would on learning that a member of the family had joined a bizarre new cult which required members to drop their careers and withdraw from their families—with the added fact that membership in the cult was against the law and punishable by death.

So, when Paul wrote that entering the Christian community is like dying, that being baptized is like being buried, he and his first readers knew that he was not exaggerating. When someone was baptized, his or her old life was over and done with, past and finished; when the new Christian emerged from the waters of baptism he or she was a new person, living a new life with new responsibilities, new values, new perspectives and new relationships within a new family. The Christian community emphasized this theme of life and death decision-making in the way it celebrated the ritual of baptism.

Consider the image of water throughout the Scriptures. In Israel's experience water is a double-edged sword. On the one hand, water is life-giving, but on the other hand it is terribly dangerous, even deadly. To understand why this is so, we must recognize that the description of Israel as a land flowing with milk and honey is an exaggeration, to say the least. In antiquity Israel was the edge of a desert, and as people who lived on the edge of a desert the Israelites appreciated how precious water was. Without a reliable source of water the crops failed, the herds died and the people perished. The most wonderful description of a truly good place that Israelites could imagine, their picture of paradise, the garden of Eden, was an oasis with not one but four streams flowing through it (Genesis 2:10). Thus water was a great blessing. The just person is compared to a tree planted near running water (Psalm 1:3). By contrast, those who are evil are like plants that have no water. They dry up and blow away in a day. Water effectively equals life. One can easily understand how that would be true for people who live on the verge of a desert.

One hears much about the Israelite army in the Hebrew scriptures but virtually nothing about an Israelite navy. This is not surprising: the Israelites were not a sea-going people. There was not one good harbor on the whole coast of ancient Israel. And like so many people who never have occasion to venture out on the waters, the Israelites found the sea very frightening. So when the biblical authors describe the chaos out of which God brings creation they turn to the image of a great formless mass of water (Genesis 1:1; Proverbs 8:22ff). When they describe the near-destruction of the world because of its sinfulness, they think of a great flood (Genesis 7:17ff). The greatest sign of God's saving action for His people was to part the sea and lead the Israelites through it while allowing the sea to roll back and destroy the Egyptians (Exodus 14:15ff). And in the rather funny story tale of Jonah, the prophet who does not want to prophesy, the point of Jonah's desperation to avoid fulfilling God's command that he go to Nineveh and call that city to repentance is made by the fact that Jonah chose to go to sea. That must have been a sure sign to any ancient Israelite that Jonah was going to come to a bad end. They knew that if you sail out to sea something terrible could easily happen to you—like being swallowed up by a great fish (Jonah 1—2). Water is a double-edged biblical symbol, both life-giving and death-dealing.

That paradoxical double-edged quality is what made water so appropriate a symbol for entry into the Christian community. This is why, when a candidate was to be brought into the church, he or she descended into water. The person was submerged in it, returned to the ancient waters of chaos, went back into the destroying waters of Noah's flood, drowned in the waters that rolled over the Egyptian army; they died. And then they re-emerged from the water, like Israel being led through the Red Sea, like Noah being saved in the ark floating on the water, like the universe being called out of the watery chaos; the new Christian emerged into new life. The newly baptized emerged from the waters of the church's womb. This is why Christians have spoken of "Mother Church"—because we have been brought to life in the church's womb, the baptismal font. Thus the imagery of the baptismal ceremony tells us that entry into the community of faith is a life-and-death moment. The old person is gone, and a new person has come into existence. Thus we customarily give a person a new name at baptism because he or she is a new person who has emerged from the womb of the baptismal font. The person they were has died, and a new person living a new life has been brought into being.

I suspect that few of us reflect on the radical quality of our baptism. Most of us have no personal memory of being baptized since we were christened when we were a few days or weeks old. Even when we attend someone else's baptism, most often an infant's, we tend to see baptism as a celebration of birth rather than a passage from death to new life. We might better understand how radical the decision to be baptized is if we think about the promises that we make at baptism.

After we have been asked to reject evil, the first of the baptismal questions that the church asks us may seem like a straightforward inquiry about our belief in a proposition about God: Do you believe in God the Father, the maker of heaven and earth? The real import of that question, however, the point at which it becomes difficult is when we realize what it implies. Do you believe that there is a maker of heaven and earth? That is to say, do you believe that there is one who made you, someone who gives your life its purpose and meaning? Do you believe that there is someone who assigns the end and goal of your existence and that you are not that some-one? Do you believe in God, and do you believe that *you* are not that God? That is a very much more challenging question than simply whether or not you accept the proposition that God exists. It is a question of whether or not you accept that your life has purpose but that *you* are not the one who assigns the purpose. The question asks whether you can live in a world that is not *your* world to do with as you choose. Can you live in a universe that is not designed by you for your own goals and purposes?

The second baptismal question: Do you believe in God the Son who has become flesh and who lived and suffered and died and was raised again in glory and now reigns with the Father in heaven? Do you believe that, although you are not God, the one who is equal to God did not think being in the form of God was anything to be clung to, but emptied himself, taking on the form of a servant and becoming human like all other human beings (Philippians 2:6–7)? Can you believe that what you are, a creature, is so powerful, so important, so wonderful that God has chosen to be a creature along with you?

And the third question: Do you believe in the Holy Spirit and in one holy Catholic church? The fact that the Spirit and the church are linked in this third question is significant. Do you believe that the Spirit of God is present in the world, not first and foremost in *you* or in *me,* but first and foremost in *us*? This is to ask, do you believe that the Spirit dwells primarily not in individuals but rather in the *community*? These are three very sweeping, very important questions. And to say "I do" to all three questions is to make a very radical statement about who God is, who I am, and what my relationship is to you and to all other human beings. To respond affirmatively to the baptismal questions underscores how radical a decision baptism is.

Because baptism is the entry into a new and strenuous life, the church anoints the newly baptized. Anointing in the ancient world was a sign of blessing and strengthening by God. Athletes were rubbed down with oil before beginning a contest, kings were anointed before undertaking their leadership role, and high priests in Israel were anointed as a sign of God's blessing. The prophets were anointed, at least figuratively, in order to prepare them to speak God's word. And we, too, have been anointed; we have become "anointed ones," "Christs." We become little Christs, literally "Christians," through baptism when we are anointed to begin the new, strenuous, demanding vocation of living the Christian life.

That anointing which takes place at baptism is completed, for most of us, some years later at confirmation. It is important to recognize that in the sacrament of confirmation it is not we who confirm anything to God, not we who attest to our baptismal promises once again, but rather God who reaffirms to us the new life which has been given us in baptism. Confirmation reaffirms what has already been celebrated in baptism: the presence of God in our lives so that we can live the life of God in the world, with all the demands, all the challenges and all the strength of that new life. Baptism is not a once-and-for-all experience. We are more baptized every day of our lives. Again and again we reconfirm our baptismal commitment. At the beginning of the eucharistic liturgy the rite of the asperges, when we are sprinkled with water, is a reminder of our baptism. So, too, it has long been a custom for people to bless themselves with holy water when entering a church. These are reminders and reaffirmations of our baptism. We must commit ourselves to baptism again and again. At every stage of our lives, in every new relationship within our lives, we discover anew what baptism really demands of us. We come to recognize new challenges, new requirements of the baptismal life. We discover what it now costs—and it always costs more than we expected—to live as a Christian. Fifty years after you were baptized you should be fifty years more really baptized then the day the water was poured on your head. Our being baptized goes on and on and on and is never finished until we have been fully, completely, raised with Christ. You see, it turns out Saint Paul was very accurate when he described becoming a Christian as dying and rising again.

For Reflection

- *In the early church, baptism often meant rejection in the secular, pagan world. Has your baptism ever put you at odds with your culture?*

- *Baptism is not a once-and-for-all experience. Have you ever had an experience where you felt your baptismal commitment was deepened?*

- *What does it mean to believe in a God that is not you? What does it mean to believe in your own holiness and goodness?*

CHAPTER SEVEN
Euc h a r i s t

*T*he Eucharist makes us who we are and tells us where we are going. The Eucharist both forms the church into a community, brings us together as a people, and reveals to us the destiny to which God calls us. If we were able to ask our earliest brothers and sisters in the faith what they thought they were doing when they celebrated the Eucharist, they would have responded that they were sealing the covenant. Covenant is the context in which the early church spoke about and tried to understand the mystery that they celebrated when they came together to eat the Lord's Supper. "Covenant" is a very ancient and rich term in the Jewish tradition. Several covenants are formed between God and his people throughout the Hebrew Bible. I will concentrate especially on three

59

great covenants that were central to Israel's understanding of its relationship to God.

The formation of the first of these three covenants concludes the story of Noah in the book of Genesis 8:20–9:17. After the waters of the great flood had subsided and the ark had come to rest on dry land, God proposes to form a covenant with Noah and his descendents. So God instructs Noah to build an altar and to choose animals for sacrifice from among those that were with him in the ark. Parts of the sacrificed animals were burned completely; that was God's share of the meal. The rest of the sacrificed meat was consumed by Noah and his family. Symbolically God and Noah and his family have eaten a meal together. The covenant between God and Noah's descendents is sealed in the blood of those sacrificed animals. The sign of this covenant with Noah is the rainbow in the sky, the visible reminder of the pact. Whenever the rainbow appears, God and all living creatures will be reminded of God's promise never again to destroy the earth with a great flood. Notice several things about this covenant story. First, God does all of the talking; God proposes the covenant and establishes its terms. Second, notice with whom the covenant is made: Noah and all his descendants, which means all of the human race since, according to the story, Noah and his family are the only survivors of the flood. Third, notice the importance of the communion meal symbolically shared by God and the human beings who are present. Fourth, notice the (implied) importance of blood in sealing the covenant. Finally, notice that the sign of the covenant is the rainbow, an external reality, outside the human beings.

The second of the great covenants, that between God and Abraham, is found just a few chapters after the story of Noah. Abraham and Sarah (or Abram and Sarai, as they are called at this point in the story) had been promised by God that if they left their own land, entered the land of Canaan and remained faithful to God that God would raise up a great people from among their descendants who would inherit the land. But Abraham and Sarah have grown old and have no children as yet. They cannot understand how God will make their descendants a great nation when they have not a single descendant as yet. So God proposes to form a covenant to reaffirm the promise to Abraham and Sarah. In the fifteenth chapter of Genesis, God instructs Abraham to take a number of animals, cut them in half and arrange the halved carcasses in two rows. Then God appears as a flaming fire which marches up and down between the slaughtered animals—apparently a kind of dramatic ancient way of saying, "If I fail to keep my promise, may I end up like these animals." The covenant is formed in the blood of those slaughtered animals. This time, however, the covenant is more explicit. No longer is the covenant made between God and all the peoples of the earth, as it had been with Noah. Now the covenant is between God and the descendants of this particular couple, Abraham and Sarah. The terms of the covenant, too, are more explicit: in brief, you will be my people, I will be your God, and therefore you will inherit this land. Finally, the sign of the covenant is much more personal:

circumcision. The sign of the covenant has changed from a natural phenomenon located outside those making the covenant, the rainbow, to a physical operation performed on the bodies of those (at least, the males) who participate in the covenant.

The third covenant story and the most famous is that of the covenant between God and Israel mediated by Moses at Sinai (Exodus 24:1–11). After the people of Israel have been led out of Egypt and have arrived at the mountain of God, Moses goes up the mountain to receive God's law, the terms of this covenant, now very elaborate and explicit indeed. Coming down the mountain, Moses reads these terms of the covenant to the assembled twelve tribes of Israel who are about to become one nation by sealing this covenant with God and with one another. Once the law has been read to them, the people express their willingness to abide by those terms. So Moses directs leaders of the Israelites to assemble stones to build an altar. Animals are sacrificed and the blood of these animals is collected in basins. Moses pours half of the blood over the altar, which is the sign of God's presence. He then sprinkles the remaining blood on the members of the tribes. This is a symbolic way of saying that God and His people have entered into a blood relationship with one another since blood is the seat of life. They share the same life in the sealing of this covenant through the blood of the sacrificed animals. In fact, just before Moses sprinkles the people with the blood, he presents the basin with the blood in it with the words, "See the blood of the covenant" (24:8). All then unite in a communion sacrifice. Notice that the sign of this covenant has moved from the rainbow or a physical change in the bodies of the participants in the covenant to changed behavior, a new way of living. The sign of the Mosaic covenant will be that those who are its members will keep the law given them by God. The sign of this covenant will be how they live.

In the books of the later prophets, beginning with Jeremiah especially, the emphasis shifts from resealing the covenant with Moses to a new covenant which God will bring about through a mediator whom he will send, someone *anointed* to be a new Moses, a *messiah* in Hebrew or a *christ* in Greek. Thus, for century after century the expectation among the Jewish people was that, when the messiah came, he would give them a new covenant with God. It was a common expectation that this new covenant would be sealed at the celebration of the old covenant, that is, at the Passover. Therefore, when on one Passover evening in Jerusalem, in an upper room, a group of people gathered together under the leadership of a wandering rabbi from Galilee whom they had come to believe might be the messiah, and heard that rabbi say to them, "I have eagerly desired to eat this Passover with you" (Luke 22:15), they certainly must have thought, "At last! This is the moment. Now Jesus will give us the new covenant." And that is exactly what Jesus did at the Last Supper.

He celebrated the Passover ritual with his disciples but changed the words and so the meaning of the celebration. He took the bread, participation in which symbolized joining together in the former covenant, and said, "This is my body," so that now, in this new communion, one actually eats the body of the Lord and so takes part in a true communion meal with God and with one another. Later in the meal he took a cup and said, echoing Moses' words at Sinai, "This is the blood of the new covenant." Now, however, the blood is not sprinkled on those who join in the sealing of the covenant but drunk by them; we actually consume that shared life and so take it within us. The blood relationship with the Lord, previously symbolized by the blood of sacrificed bulls and goats, is truly established through the Eucharist. And the sign of this new covenant established between God and his people is that they love one another. The covenant sign has moved from being the rainbow, to the physical change of circumcision, to a changed form of behavior, living the law, to a changed motive for living the law. "I give you a new commandment, that you love one another. Just as I have loved you, you also should love one another. By this everyone will know that you are my disciples, if you have love for one another" (John 13:34–35). The sign of discipleship, the sign of membership in the new covenant, is that we love one another as Jesus has loved us. Just as the covenant brought by Moses not only established the bond between God and his people but turned twelve tribes into one nation, so in the Eucharist, we are not only joined with God but are formed together into one community. The Eucharist truly makes the church. In signing our covenant with God, in sealing it again and again each time we celebrate the Eucharist, we are joined to one another and to God. The Eucharist makes us into *a people* and so enables us to be the people *of God*. The Eucharist makes us who we are. It is the sealing of the New Covenant, celebrated again and again and again.

Not only does the Eucharist make us who we are, it tells us where we are going. I suspect that if we could find someone who had never heard of Christianity and so knew nothing about the Eucharist, and invited that person to attend a celebration of the Eucharist and afterward asked what he or she thought of the ritual, such a person might well reply, "Well, you Christians certainly make a great deal of fuss about eating a little bit of bread and drinking some wine together." And the person would be correct, of course. The eucharistic celebration centers on bread that we believe becomes the body of Christ and on wine that we believe becomes the blood of Christ. Consider that bread for a moment. There is no intrinsic difference between the bread which becomes the Eucharist and the bread that we popped into the toaster at breakfast or that we will use for sandwiches at lunch. There is no intrinsic difference between the wine that will become the Eucharist and the wine that we drink with friends at dinner. If this bread can become the body of Christ, why not all that other bread? If this wine can become the blood of Christ, why not all wine? If bread grown from soil and nurtured by sunlight and watered by rain, if grapes tended by vine-dressers and grown with the help of sun and soil and rain, can become the presence of Christ, then why not the sun, the soil and the rain? Why not the vine, why not the wheat? In fact, if this tiny fragment of the material world can be transformed into the fullness of the presence of Christ, and therefore the fullness of the presence of God in human terms, then why not the whole material universe? And that is, of course, precisely the point.

In the prayers for the feast of Corpus Christi, we find an antiphon that originated in the Middle Ages, *O sacrum convivium,* "O sacred banquet." In the antiphon we describe the Eucharist as a *pignus futurae gloriae.* In Latin a *pignus* is a "down payment," a "first installment." Thus, in the liturgy of the feast of Corpus Christi, we call the Eucharist the down payment, the first installment of future glory. Precisely right: the eucharistic bread and wine are, as it were, the tip of the iceberg, the point at which we see what the whole universe is destined to become. The whole universe is destined to be transformed into the presence of Christ, the fullness of God in the flesh. The whole universe is destined to be transformed into the presence of God in Christ.

In his first letter to the church in Corinth, Saint Paul beautifully expresses the destiny of the universe when he writes,

> Then comes the end, when he hands over
> the kingdom to God the Father, after he has
> destroyed every ruler and every authority
> and power. For he must reign until he has
> put all his enemies under his feet. The last
> enemy to be destroyed is death. For "God
> has put all things in subjection under his
> feet." But when it says, "All things are put
> in subjection," it is plain that this does not
> include the one who put all things in subjec-
> tion under him. When all things are sub-

jected to him, then the Son himself will also
be subjected to the one who put all things in
subjection under him, so that God may be
all in all. (1 Corinthians 15:24–28)

That is where we are all going. That is the destiny that
the Eucharist reveals to us now: the transformation of
the universe into the presence of God, so that God may
be everything in everything. The Eucharist makes us
who we are and reveals to us where we are going. That
is why we are a eucharistic people: because we are made
into a people by the sealing of the covenant in the
Eucharist, a people who know what the destiny of the
world is. Consequently we are the people who respond by
saying "Thank you." (The Greek word for "to say thank
you" is *eucharistein*.) We are the people who give thanks
because we are constantly the recipients of gifts. The
Eucharist makes us who we are. The Eucharist reveals
our destiny.

For Reflection

- *What is a covenant? How is the Eucharist the new covenant?*

- *What does "Real Presence" mean? Do you feel that you and God have a covenant together?*

- *How does the Eucharist point to the holiness of everything? What does that mean in terms of our commitment to creation? To one another?*

Chapter Eight

Sacraments of Vocation

*T*he Catholic Church celebrates two vocations as public sacramental moments. One of these vocations is official ministry within the church, the sacrament of Holy Orders. The other is the vocation of marriage.

Holy Orders

The fundamental sacrament of ministry in the church is baptism. In baptism we are all called to ministry. The church is not a community made up of some people who minister and others who are recipients of ministry. Everyone in the church is called to ministry in some way or other. But because everyone is called to ministry, some people are called to be public embodiments of ministry. There are many responsibilities which the church must fulfill at different times and on various levels in its life. Three responsibilities, however, are always and every-where present in the church's life. One cannot even imagine calling a community the church if it is not attending to these three responsibilities.

The first of these responsibilities is that of holding the community together. A community unconcerned about maintaining unity among its members, a commu-nity that had no interest in other Christian communi-ties, could not be described as a church. A community with no interest in maintaining communion simply is not the church of Christ.

The second responsibility always and everywhere present in the church is responsibility to and for the Word of God. By the Word of God I intend Scripture to be sure, but also the whole living out of the message of Scripture in worship and action, in reflection and prayer—in other words, tradition. A community that had no concern about passing on the tradition of the Word of God, that had no interest in exploring or learning about that tradition of the Word of God, cannot be called the church.

Thirdly, there is a responsibility of direct service to those in need both within the community and outside it. A community that could deny that it has any responsi-bility to care for the needs of others, whether they are members of the community or not, does not deserve the name of church.

These three responsibilities are present in the church on all its levels—from the domestic church of the household to the universal church, and in every age of its life. Who is called to meet these responsibilities?

Everyone is called by baptism to all three tasks. All of us have a responsibility to maintain the communion of the church. All of us have a responsibility to learn, reflect upon and pass on to others the Word of God. And all of us have a responsibility to serve the needs of our brothers and sisters within the church and outside it.

What can we call these three responsibilities? I suggest that there are ancient and familiar names for these three roles within the church's life. The responsibility to hold the community together is *episcopacy*. The responsibility to and for the word of God is *presbyterate* or priesthood. The responsibility to serve the needs of others inside and outside the church is *diakonia,* diaconate. Consequently, I suggest that there is by baptism a universal episcopate, a universal presbyterate and a universal diaconate. Everyone is called by baptism to these three roles in the church's life. But if *everyone* is called to these roles, *someone* must embody one or other of these roles full time and permanently. That is what we mean by ordination. The sacramental principle is that what is always and everywhere the case must be embodied and expressed somewhere sometime. If we apply that principle to ministry in the church, we must say that, if everyone is called to the episcopate by baptism, someone must live it out that call publicly in order to remind the rest of us what we are called to by baptism. If everyone is called to the presbyterate, someone must live out that ministry full time and publicly in order to sacramentalize it for the rest of us. If everyone is called to the ministry of diaconal service, then someone must embody that role of diaconal service in a public and permanent way as a sacrament of what is true of all of us. Consequently, in the sacrament of Holy Orders the community asks certain of its members to publicly accept responsibility for one of these three obligations that always and everywhere mark the church's life and to live it out in a strikingly public way in order to be sacraments to the whole community of its baptismal call. In other words, when someone is ordained to the episcopate or the priesthood or the diaconate, that person not only receives a sacrament but becomes a sacrament. The ordained person is asked to become a living embodiment of the responsibility to preserve the communion of the church, or a living embodiment of responsibility to and for the Word of God, or a living embodiment of diaconal service to all those in need.

How one lives out these responsibilities has changed and will continue to change from one age in the church's history to another and from one place in the church's life to another. In recent decades some have described ordination as the empowerment to perform certain functions. That says something about the meaning of ordination, but I do not think it says enough. It is impossible to draw up a list of functions that have always and everywhere characterized the role of the bishop or the role of the priest or the role of the deacon. For example, we might readily think that characteristic parts of the priest's role are to preside at the celebration of Eucharist and to extend absolution in the sacrament of reconciliation. In fact, however, we know that, for several centuries, most priests did not preside at the Eucharist. The usual presider at eucharistic celebrations was the bishop, not the priest. Likewise, for centuries, the person who extended absolution in the sacrament of reconciliation was the bishop, not the priest. So it is difficult, if not impossible, to draw up a list of functions that were always exclusively episcopal functions or presbyteral functions or diaconal functions, and to make the performance of those functions the hallmark of being a bishop, a priest or a deacon. That is why I think that it is much more in accord with historical evidence of the church's life to speak of three responsibilities which may entail different functions at different times and places. The responsibilities remain constant: the responsibility of holding the community together, the responsibility to and for the Word of God, and the responsibility of diaconal service.

One cannot possibly understand the sacrament of Holy Orders without seeing that it is built on the sacrament of baptism. It would be an immense mistake to oppose the ministry of the ordained to the ministry of all the baptized, because what makes one an ordained minister is the commission to sacramentalize the ministry of all the baptized. If one wants to reaffirm the importance of a sacrament, work to strengthen the reality that the sacrament points to and embodies. Thus the best, truest and most effective way to reaffirm the importance of ordained ministry is to strengthen the ministry of all the baptized. The more richly that all of us as members of the church recognize our call to ministry the more sense the ministry of the ordained makes within that community. The more the church recognizes itself as a community of ministers, the more it can recognize the value, the dignity and the importance of ordained ministry within the church. The ministry of all the baptized and ordained ministry are not in competition: they constantly complement and reinforce one another. The ministry of the ordained sacramentalizes the ministry of the baptized.

Marriage

Marriage occupies a unique position within the Christian tradition. In some ways it is not like the other six public, communal sacraments. The other six sacraments make sense only within the context of Christianity. Marriage, of course, existed prior to the Christian tradition and exists outside the Christian tradition. What is there about the human relationship of marriage that has led Christians to recognize that it is a sacrament? After all, there are other deep and vital human relationships which might claim sacramental status, for example, parenthood. Why is marriage one of the public manifestations of the presence of grace in the world? Is there something intrinsic to the human reality of marriage that makes it apt to be recognized as sacramental? I think the answer is very definitely yes. After all, the sign of the presence of grace is the capacity to give oneself away. If grace is God's love outside the Trinity, then the evidence of grace is the capacity to give oneself away in agapic love. Wherever we see the gift of self to another we glimpse the presence of God; we see the reality of grace.

Sometimes that self-gift is not explicitly named as grace. For example, in the Gospel of Matthew 25 we have the depiction of the Last Judgment. The Son of Man comes in triumph and glory at the end of time, mounts the throne of judgment and gathers all nations to be judged. He separates them out as one might separate sheep from goats. The Son of Man tells the sheep on his right hand that they are blessed because they cared for him when he was hungry and thirsty, when he was naked and imprisoned, when he was sick and homeless. Those on his right ask in response when they encountered him in such conditions. He replies that, when they acted in behalf of the least of his brothers and sisters, they acted for him. Then the Son of Man tells those on his left that they stand condemned because they ignored him when he was hungry and thirty, naked and homeless, sick and imprisoned. They protest that they never saw him in such conditions and ignored him. And the reply is that when they neglected to act for the least of his brothers and sisters they neglected him (Matthew 25:31–46). The most obvious meaning of this story is that caring for one's brothers or sisters, especially "the least" of them, is caring for the Lord. Loving our neighbor is our experience of loving the Lord. One cannot separate the love of God and the love of neighbor. This is profoundly true. But there is a further point to the story, one not always noticed: we may not accurately name loving our neighbor as loving God. Notice that both the sheep, the blessed on the right, and the goats, the condemned on the left, respond that they did not recognize the Son of Man when they acted or failed to act in response to their brothers and sisters in need. Those who are blessed because they loved their brothers and sisters admit that they did not act for the Son of Man's sake, that they were not thinking of him and did not recognize him when they reached out in love to their brothers and sisters. The point of the Son of Man's response to them is, "Whether you did it for me or not, you did it, and that is what matters." So it is possible not to realize the full depth of what we are doing when we love our brothers and sisters. Nevertheless, whenever we genuinely love others, whenever we give ourselves away to others, whenever we reach out in service to someone else, we are loving God.

In the last supper discourse in John's Gospel, Jesus says to his followers, "No one has greater love than this, to lay down one's life for one's friends" (John 15:13). We human beings know one extraordinary relationship in which we attempt to give ourselves away to another as deeply, fully, richly as possible; that relationship is marriage. In marriage two people give themselves to one another on every level of their being—physically and emotionally, familially and financially, spiritually and psychologically. On every level two people give themselves to one another and promise to do so permanently. They vow that they will attempt to live this life of self-gift to and with one another forever. There is no richer expression of human love, no deeper, fuller manifestation of agape between human beings, than marriage truly and fully lived. And for that reason every marriage is incipiently sacramental. The Christian tradition recognizes the grace which is present in every true, vital and living marriage. Thus the sacrament of Christian marriage is the community's public celebration of what is true of every real marriage: the manifestation of grace. The sacrament of marriage is recognition of the presence of God's agape in our midst. To see a marriage lived well is to see the presence of the grace of God manifested in the flesh. It is to glimpse who God is: the one who gives himself away perfectly.

A full Christian theology of marriage will only be possible when we no longer try to understand how marriage is like the other six sacraments but rather try to understand how the other six sacraments are like marriage. For marriage is the human relationship which most fully evidences what grace calls us to: to become pure and perfect gifts to one another. That is what mirrors the grace of God.

Both marriage and Holy Orders are often referred to as sacraments of vocation. Both sacraments lead us into states of life which are ways of living out the deeper and more basic vocation of being Christian. But even being a Christian is a way of living out a more fundamental, indeed, the most fundamental vocation, that of being a human being. How can we determine the best way for each one of us to live out that all-important vocation of being as richly, fully, truly human as we can possibly be? I think that, although many factors will come into play in each individual's life, there are always three questions which we must address.

The first question is, "Is this way of living a life a source of joy for me?" Please notice: I do not say "a source of happiness," because my happiness is affected by many factors. It depends on how I slept last night, and whether breakfast agreed with me, and what the weather is like. I am speaking about joy, which is one of the fruits of the presence of the Holy Spirit. Joy is the deep inward delight that one takes in living one's life. That deep inward delight is independent of all external factors, like weather and health. Joy is a mark of making the right vocational decision. God never asks us not to be joyful.

The second question that has to be asked is, "Do I possess the skills, the talents, the gifts, which will make me good at living out this vocation?" It is not enough that we find joy in a particular decision. One also has to be good at one's vocation. After all, I may take great joy in being a brain surgeon, but if all of my patients end up incapacitated as a result of my operating on them, then I am not called to be a brain surgeon.

And the third question is, "Is this vocational choice a good way in which to give myself away to others?" Do people need and want me to choose this vocation? For example, if I live in Manhattan, although I may take great satisfaction in being a shepherd and I am very good dealing with sheep, I doubt that there is much call for a shepherd in Central Park. One must find a way of giving oneself away that is a true service to others. All vocational choices are ways of loving your neighbor because only in being so can they genuinely be embraced as calls from God.

For Reflection

- *What does it mean that we are all called to ministry?*

- *What does that mean practically in your life?*

- *"God never asks us not to be joyful." What do you think of this statement?"*

- *How are you giving your life away?*

CHAPTER NINE

Reconciliation

*I*t will certainly be no surprise to you to learn that most
Catholics' experience of the sacrament of reconciliation
has changed dramatically in last thirty years. At one
time, it was common practice for many Catholics to celebrate the sacrament of reconciliation—we usually spoke
of it as going to confession—once or twice a month, perhaps even once a week. Now these same Catholics or
their children find it no surprise to discover that they
have not been to the sacrament of reconciliation for several months or a year. Why this change? I suspect that
there are many reasons. Indeed, one could argue that, in
the history of the church, the sacrament of reconciliation
has been a kind of barometer. Whenever the church has
passed through a period of rethinking its mission, one

place that this rethinking shows up most sharply and clearly is in the way people celebrate the sacrament of reconciliation. It certainly has been the case that since Vatican II the church has extensively rethought its nature and its mission, and so we should not be surprised to find that the way in which most Catholics experience reconciliation has also changed a great deal.

One way to consider the sacrament of reconciliation today would be to address the question most often asked by Catholics about the sacrament at the present time. That question is, "What do we need the priest for? Why can't we pray to our ever loving and merciful Father, admit our sinfulness, ask for forgiveness and be assured of that forgiveness in our lives? Why do we need to confess to a priest? Why do we need a priest to assure us of God's forgiveness?" It is all well and good to reply that the church understands the sacrament to have been established in this way in accord with the intention of Christ, but that only moves the question back one stage. Then the question would be, "Why is it the intention of Christ that the sacrament be arranged this way?" I think that this is a very important question because it points to a serious misunderstanding about the nature of sin.

The assumption underlying the often-asked question about reconciliation seems to be that sin separates us from God and that it is our relationship with God which needs to be healed. If that were the case, then it would be quite true that we do not need the presence of another human being. We could simply confess directly to God and be assured of God's forgiveness. But sin does not separate us from God alone. Sin separates us from one another, and that is a very important consideration. We tend to assume that sin is an obstacle between God and me. In fact sin is a radical injustice that I have done to you as well as an obstacle that I have placed to my relationship to God.

Let me suggest an example that I first used years ago in talking with young children preparing for the sacrament of reconciliation. Pardon me if it seems somewhat too simple. Think of people working together on an assembly line in a factory. Each person on that assembly line has his or her own particular task to perform that contributes to making the finished product. Each one has to presume that all the others on the assembly line are working as fast and efficiently as they can. For if nine out of ten people on that assembly line did exactly what they were suppose to do while the tenth one neglected to fulfill his or her task, at the end the finished product would be junk. The one person who neglected to fulfill his or her role would destroy the good work of all the other members of the assembly line who had been working as hard as they could. One can say much the same about the effect of sin on the life of church. Each of us is called to a unique role in fulfilling the church's mission. The church's role in the world is to make Christ fully present at all times and in all places. Each member of the church makes Christ present in a unique and special way. For each of us is related to others in a way that no one else is. I am related to my parents, my brother, my sister, my niece, my nephew, my students, my colleagues in a way no one else is, and you are related to your family and friends and colleagues in ways that I am not. So if my parents are going to find Christ present in their eldest son, if my brother and sister are going to see Christ in their older brother, if my niece and nephew are to discover Christ present in their uncle, if my friends are to meet Christ in their friend, I must make Christ present because no one else stands in precisely those roles to those people. If you are to make Christ present to your family and friends and colleagues, only you can do so, for neither I nor anyone else occupies your position in relationship to those people. This means that if I fail to make Christ clearly and truly present in my life, part of the church's mission of making Christ present at all times and in all places to all people will not be accomplished. And if I fail to accomplish my part of the work of the church, the work of God's people is impaired. My failure to make Christ fully present in all the relationships of my life weakens your work as part of the church. My sinfulness diminishes your work. Each one of us by our failure to live the Christian life as fully and deeply as possible undermines the mission of the church to which we are all called by baptism. The sinfulness of each hurts all. Therefore we need to be reconciled with one another. Thus, when we come to the sacrament of reconciliation, we are not only reconciled with God but with the church, the rest of the community. This is why the priest must be present in the sacrament of reconciliation, not first and foremost as a spokesperson for God but as the representative of the community. Because I am reconciled with the members of the church through the representative of the community, I am also restored to full communion with the head of the community, Christ. By being reconciled with one another we return to full communion with God. Unless we understand the social significance of our sins, we cannot begin to understand the social dimension of our reconciliation with one another.

Reconciliation is never a wiping away of the past. We never simply obliterate our sinfulness. Rather, we catch that sinfulness up into a new and wider experience of the love of God and of our communion with one another. In his *Confessions,* after completing the narrative of his early sinful life and his subsequent conversion, Saint Augustine raised an interesting question. He asked whether it was a good thing that he had written the narrative. For if he had come to regret deeply his sinful past and believed that God had forgiven him, what was the point in remembering that past? Should it not simply be obliterated? Should he not simply put his past behind him and forget it? Augustine's answer is profound. He recognized that his sinfulness had led him to recognize the love of God, that only when he realized the depth of sin's presence in his life was he able to see who God is and how God worked in his life. Indeed, Augustine was convinced that recalling his sinfulness was a necessary part of his praise of God throughout his *Confessions.* How could he praise God as his savior without remembering what God had saved him from? So Augustine recognized that reconciliation is not a matter of wiping the slate clean so that one can start afresh as though the past had never happened. Reconciliation is seeing the whole of one's past life from a new angle. It is a re-envisioning of who one is and how one lives in a new context. It is seeing one's selfishness, one's blindness, one's sinfulness as loved and embraced by God so that the very meaning of that sinfulness is changed.

Year after year at the Easter vigil we celebrate this insight of Augustine's when we hear the *Exultet* sung, the proclamation of the Lord's Resurrection. In this Easter proclamation, the church exclaims, "O happy fault, O necessary sin of Adam!" These are Augustine's words taken from one of his Easter sermons. Here we have one of the Fathers of the church calling the fall of humanity a happy event. Why? Certainly not because Augustine in any way downplays the evil of sin. His point, which the church has adopted as its own in the Easter proclamation, is that even the depth of evil is transformed by the extraordinary gift of God's love manifested in the Incarnation and Redemption. Because of that manifestation of love even sinfulness can now be celebrated. We can actually celebrate our sinfulness because the love of God so utterly surpasses our capacity for evil. As Saint Paul says, "[B]ut where sin increased, grace abounded all the more" (Romans 5:20).

It is that conviction, that great Augustinian insight, which allows us to *celebrate* reconciliation, to make it into an occasion of joy in the life of the church and in our own lives. The sacrament of reconciliation is not an occasion for mourning. It is not about how wicked I have been but about how good God is. Like all sacraments, reconciliation is not primarily about *my* action, whether good or bad, but about *God's* action. Were we to recognize that, the sacrament of reconciliation might no longer be perceived as a burden that we must be willing to shoulder periodically. Instead, it would become a source of joy as the community acknowledges that all have sinned and all are forgiven because all are embraced by the love of God.

My sinful brothers and sisters, we have all been condemned justly. But even more importantly, my redeemed brothers and sisters, we can all be reconciled. That is what demands to be celebrated. If we recognize the communal dimension of our sinfulness and our reconciliation, and acknowledge that what is being celebrated is not the depth of our sins but the height of God's love, then the sacrament of reconciliation might yet have a new birth in our church.

For Reflection

• *Why do we need a priest in the sacrament of reconciliation?*

• *How is the sacrament of reconciliation more about God than it is about us?*

• *What is your attitude toward the sacrament of reconciliation?*

Chapter Ten
Tradition

When I was growing up in Brooklyn in the 1950s, very few words were used by Catholics as frequently as the word "tradition." Tradition seems to have meant for most Catholics the story of how nothing had changed in the course of nineteen hundred years. Essentially everything we did and said and the ways we prayed were what Christians had said and done and the ways in which they had prayed since the time of Jesus. Tradition meant that, over the course of centuries, nothing changed. Now, while it is certainly true that there is continuity between our age and Jesus' time, the word "tradition" really designates the movement of passing on the faith from one generation, one time and place, to another. Therefore the real meaning of tradition is not a story of how nothing has changed but a story of movement and change and growth and development. That is a big shift in the way in which Catholics use the word. In the course of the last quarter-century some Catholics have found the shift disconcerting. Indeed, some Catholics seem to think that the way in which to guard the tradition is to make certain that nothing does change. In fact, that is the way to betray the tradition. Cardinal John Henry Newman, the great nineteenth-century Catholic convert and theologian, wrote in his *Essay on the Development of Christian Doctrine* that "in a higher world it is otherwise, but here below to live is to change, and to be perfect is to have changed often."

In order to say what one has always said it is frequently necessary to say it in a new way. It may prove necessary to say it in many new ways over a long period of time. Let me offer an example. Imagine that the manager of a store famous for always being in the forefront of fashion decides that the best way to keep the store at the forefront of fashion is to make certain that no one ever changes the displays in the store windows again. Here you see the misuse of tradition. In order to stay where one has always been, one must change constantly. If the manager of our imaginary store wants to be sure that the store remains at the forefront of fashion, he or she will have to change what appears in the store windows frequently. One of the best statements about tradition that I know is found in Lewis Carroll's *Through The Looking Glass*. In chapter 2, while talking with the Red Queen, Alice and the Queen begin to run. They run and run and run, and the Red Queen keeps urging her to go faster, faster, faster, faster. Finally, when Alice can scarcely go another step, the Queen stops. As Alice looks around she is surprised to find that they are precisely where they were when they started running. The Red Queen tells her that "it takes all the running you can do, to keep in the same place. If you want to get somewhere else, you must run at least twice as fast as that!" So, too, in order to remain faithful to the tradition, in order to stay where we have been, we must change as fast as we can. The story of the tradition is the story of how the church has run—and changed—as fast as it can for nearly two thousand years. Any attempt to freeze-frame that story, to turn a motion picture into a photograph, is to betray tradition, not to keep it alive.

To understand tradition, therefore, it is helpful to consider two closely related ideas often spoken about among Catholics. One is the ancient image of the communion of saints. The other is an idea that only began to be widely accepted by Catholics thanks to the influence of Cardinal Newman in the nineteenth century, the idea of the development of doctrine, that doctrine grows and changes and develops in the course of the church's life.

To understand the communion of saints, we must put aside the idea of that communion as a savings-and-loan association to which some, those here in this life, still contribute, while others, the saints, have retired to a sort of spiritual Florida with lots of capital in the bank, and still others, those in purgatory, have unfortunately gone bankrupt en route. We contribute capital to this savings-and-loan association, and the director of the bank, God, channels some of those funds along with all that has been stored up by the saints to the bankrupt in purgatory, who will in turn contribute to us should we need assistance now or in the future. This rather mythological notion of the communion of saints may serve a purpose, but I do not think it is very helpful in the long run. A far better way to think about the communion of saints is to take "communion" in its original sense of conversation, i.e., talking with one another. To become part of the communion of saints is to enter a conversation between the living and the dead which has gone on for almost twenty centuries. Indeed, if we think of those whom Saint Augustine described as the saints of the first dispensation—Abraham and Isaac and Jacob, Sara and Rebecca and Rachel—then the communion of saints extends a great deal longer than two thousand years. In this conversation people who have lived at different times in the church's life, in different cultures and different places have the opportunity to exchange with one another. Such conversation is what prevents us from falling into what G. K. Chesterton, the delightful Catholic thinker and essayist in the first half of the twentieth century, described as "the most degrading of all forms of servitude," namely, being merely a child of one's time. The communion of saints prevents us from being merely twenty-first-century North Americans because we are in communion with people who are not North Americans and who do not live in the twenty-first century. The communion of saints is a conversation across time and across geography that allows tradition to remain rich and vital and the faith to be passed from one period to another.

As the faith is passed, it must be reexpressed, because the insights, the styles of prayer, the ways of

Christian living, the kinds of community, the sort of liturgy that we celebrate together, change. What was beautiful in Europe in the Middle Ages may not be appropriate for Africa in the twenty-first century. What was splendid for Catholics in North America in the twentieth century might have been quite unintelligible to Catholics in Latin America in the seventeenth century. Different times and places require different ways of saying the same thing. That is what I mean by development of doctrine. It is what Newman meant when he wrote that "to live is to change, and to be perfect is to have changed often." In order to fully explore the enormous richness of the Mystery of God revealed to us in the life and death and destiny of Jesus of Nazareth and which continues in our own lives individually and communally because of the presence of the Holy Spirit requires the entire history of humanity. In no one time or place can the fullness of that Mystery find expression in one particular doctrinal formula or system of religious education or way of prayer or style of life. The Mystery requires the full range of human experience, which is why each generation must be willing to enter into conversation with the generations before it. We are never free to start fresh in the church. But neither are we free to stand pat in the church. This conversation, the communion of saints, prevents the tradition from devolving into strange aberrations and cranky forms of superstition. In every generation women and men of faith must set out together to explore the richness of the Mystery, not just by thinking and talking about it but by attempting to pray it and live it. Sharing that experience with one another in our own time and place and comparing our way of living as church with previous times and places allows us to say that we are part of the tradition.

It is never enough, therefore, simply to hold to the faith or maintain the faith or keep the faith, because the only way in which we can truly live the faith is by developing the faith, passing on the faith and allowing the faith to grow with our own experience and the experience of our contemporaries. This requires great discernment on the part of all believers. It is that process of discernment that goes on in the church's magisterium. Magisterium does not mean that there are some persons in the church who, by the grace of office, have a privileged access to the truth of the faith and who in some miraculous fashion fathom the faith fully. Magisterium means that there are those within the community who are charged with maintaining the conversation, keeping it open and alive, never permitting any one generation, any one time or place to separate itself from the communion of saints. This is why those in the community who are especially charged with maintaining the unity of the community exercise the office of magisterium, namely, the college of bishops throughout the world with the bishop of Rome, the pope, as its head. The magisterium is certainly not a doctrinal yardstick against which everyone else's expression of the faith and way of living the faith is measured. The magisterium keeps the conversation alive. Once again we are dealing with a story of growth and change and development, not a story of stasis and standing pat.

Thus the idea of development of doctrine, which

Newman and other nineteenth-century thinkers made familiar to the Catholic community, is not a responsibility of any one group in the church. It is not the unique province of bishops or theologians; it is the work of the whole people of God. Every time someone preaches a homily or teaches a religion class, every time parents teach their children to pray, every time we come together to celebrate the Eucharist, every time a theologian writes, every time a bishop addresses his diocese, every time a pope speaks to the universal church, doctrine develops. Some developments will prove fruitful; some developments may be tried and found wanting. But doctrinal development goes forward continually. The worst disservice that we can do in our time to fidelity to the Catholic tradition would be to try to freeze that tradition. Any attempt to stop the development of doctrine, any attempt to make the way in which the Mystery has been praised and lived in a particular time and a particular place into the final and finished form of the Mystery, is idolatry. It is to fall into the mistake of reducing God to one particular form of our experience of God. Sadly, people sometimes invoke tradition today in ways that betray tradition.

The distinguished historical theologian Jaroslav Pelikan offers a splendid summary of what I am suggesting. Pelikan writes: "Tradition is the living faith of the dead, traditionalism is the dead faith of the living."[4] It is our responsibility to see that the faith of all of the men and women of the community who have gone before

[4] Jaroslav Pelikan, *The Vindication of Tradition* (New Haven, Conn.: Yale University Press, 1984), p. 65.

us, with whom we are in conversation in the communion of saints, is passed on as living and vital and vibrant and still developing to the generations who come after us. Any attempt to reduce the faith to what we were taught in catechism classes or the way we celebrated when we were young or how it was when we were growing up, is to belittle the mystery. It is to make tradition into the dead faith of those now living. Traditionalism may be a very grave heresy, but tradition remains a very great gift.

For Reflection

- *People of faith never stop growing in their understanding of God. How has your image of God changed? How has that realization changed your life?*

- *Tradition depends upon the communion of saints. What insights from the past are especially important today?*

- *Why is tradition a gift and traditionalism a heresy?*

NOTES

[1] Included in a letter to Thomas Butts, November 22, 1802, in Geoffrey Keynes, ed., *Complete Prose and Poetry of William Blake* (London: The Nonesuch Press, 1989), p. 862.

[2] Nicholas Lash, *His Presence in the World: A Study in Eucharistic Worship and Theology* (London: Sheed and Ward, 1968), p. 4f: "It therefore becomes clear that the real difficulty in saying that Christianity, or theology, is about both God and man, the real difficulty in *verus Deus et verus homo,* consists not in knowing what we mean by *God* or what we mean by *man* (though these are not small questions), but in the difficulty of knowing what we mean by *and.*"

[3] John Paul II, *Redemptor Hominis* (Washington, D.C.: United States Catholic Conference, 1979), #10, p. 28: "In reality, the name for that deep amazement at the human person's worth and dignity is the Gospel, that is to say: the Good News. It is also called Christianity." As the translation of *hominis* I have substituted for "man" the more accurate "human person," which also has the advantage of being gender-inclusive.

[4] Jaroslav Pelikan, *The Vindication of Tradition* (New Haven, Connecticut: Yale University Press, 1984), p. 65.

INDEX

A
agape, 6-8
anointing
    in Baptism 56-57
    of Christ, 63
Aquinas, Saint Thomas, 15-16
ascension, 23
Augustine, Saint
    Confessions, 83
    original sin, 84
    saints of the first dispensation, 90
    trinity, 8

B
Baptism, 49-57
    anointing in, 56-57
    change of life in, 50-52
    symbolism of water and, 52-54
Blake, William, 17

C
Carroll, Lewis, 88-89
Chesterton, G. K., 90
Christ
    anointing of, 63
    presence through love, 7
church
    as community, 40-41, 45
    as holy, 45, 46
    as sacrament, 18
    need for, 39
communion of saints, 89-90
community
    and reconciliation, 81-83
    as dwelling place for the Spirit, 56
    church as, 40-41, 45
    importance of, for salvation, 37

Scripture Index